If you are reading the introduction of this book you are in the right place to reach the goal. With proven results, below.

"BECOME RICH IN 10 STEPS WITHOUT WORKING ONE DAY FOR ANYONE"

Presentation of the book

This book presents the formula that many millionaires of the world have used to become millionaires in a very short time. Money is like a cycle and has no schedules, it is printed every second.

Just by following the discipline that is presented here, in a few months you will see your money grow. It's just a matter of taking the first step.

Say no to the markets in networks that only sell dreams and enslave you for the dreams of others and yours are never realized.

The content of this book is worth gold and is focused on real stories of people who are achieving and have achieved economic success in a few months, no matter what their initial financial situation was.

Even without having anything in your pocket, it only depends on your discipline, your strength of will, a strategy that leads to materialize a great idea, effort and perseverance is all you need to achieve it. Creating a system that will give you income for the rest of your life is what you need.

The accumulated money is like a warehouse of merchandise that if you only take one day it ends; create a system that is like the current of a river, that always flows, will ensure your present and your future without sacrificing your physical effort. A good profession can lead you to have a good job that requires your presence and effort to get the money to your pocket.

Use your knowledge to create a system that ensures unlimited income for an indefinite period of time, even to your future generations without your presence being essential.

Janet Taylor

Author

1. Invest in books that teach, inspire and empower you about money

Learning how to be a millionaire does not have to be a mystery. The first thing is to clarify that it is a question of habits, and not of magic or secret formulas.

If you want to achieve your financial freedom you must change some actions of your life, have the right mentality and take the advice listed below. Some of these habits are easy; others difficult to implement that can take time.

The important thing is that you turn them part of your routine so that you begin to see how your life and personal finances improve, and the question of how to be a millionaire finds your answer.

A saving mentality is of no use if you do not focus on increasing your income; always remember that if you want something different from what you have you must do something different from what you are doing. "Doing the same, you do not get different results"

It is useless to save your money and deprive yourself of expenses, if you are not doing something productive with this money, or if worse still, you are simply putting it off to buy something in the future. To be a millionaire you must invest your savings, define a strategy.

If your number one goal is to be a millionaire, and you make it a priority, other things in your life will occupy a secondary position and you will be sending a message to the universe very clear of what you want to achieve.

The richest men in the world are not employees. They are entrepreneurs, investors and people with guts to generate new sources of income through investments, business and calculated risks.

The poor look for a job that generates money for their day-to-day expenses.

The rich create a system that generates money for it every day without having to work and instead of being employed; they look for people of poor mentality who want to be employed.

When we are employees, no matter the category of employment we will always be working for the dream of our employer. In this guide what is wanted is that you take initiative and start to pursue your own dreams.

2. It establishes a budget of expenses, income and investments:

People who have a budget show that they have control over their personal finances. They know how much money comes in, how much money goes out, how it goes out and when it comes out. It is an objective that is not measurable, realistic, measured in time, nor specific. Rather put a figure to your dream. Being a millionaire is about creating systems that do not need your presence to function.

3. Start today

Finally it begins. All these ideas and steps that answer your question of how to be a millionaire have no meaning if they do not add action, unless you make the decision and start today the million dollar life of your dreams.

The only way to change your current situation is by acting differently. If you do not feel comfortable with your present, act differently and your future will change. There is no other way.

Nor is it about taking all your money and saving it completely affecting your quality of life, if not finding a method of saving that fits your life project and financial goals.

You will not live your job all your life, if you cling to a fixed monthly salary you will go into chaos when you become unemployed, because you will not have to survive and cover your expenses for at least a good time, Imagine if you get sick and you can no longer work.

The first thing is that you have an emergency fund with an amount equal to your salary that covers at least three months. Then we advise you to seek to invest in a business, stock exchange or real estate, if you can monetize a hobby, buy and sell products or offer their services according to their skills and knowledge.

The texts are a great ally in the progress of a person, since they teach, inspire and train in different topics. Books are a source of knowledge, ideas and emotions that are very important to take advantage of.

The millionaire people know that thanks to them they have evolved professionally and have managed to generate the ideas that allowed them to reach success. The great advantage of books is that they are very accessible and you can save them and consult them whenever you need them.

However, to fulfill your dream you should at least start with an ideal of what you want to gather this year or the next three do not be afraid to set a figure. After that, divide it in months, weeks, and days to see if it is possible to fulfill it. For example, your goal may be to achieve $ 2 million in the New Year, develop a strategy that allows you to achieve them and establish an end, that is, what is that money for.

Make numbers, add, multiply, divide. It is better to earn 5 dollars 100 times than 50 dollars 3 times, if you implement a strategy of a product that has the possibility of going out a thousand times a day at a price of 2 dollars, it would be 2000 dollars a day, and if this leaves 50% of benefits would be 7,000 a week,

30,000 a month and 365,000 dollars a year.

There are no magic tricks that teach you how to get rich overnight; and as we stated in our book, this is a process that takes time, but if you follow the right advice, your personal finances will improve in a matter of days.

4. Know some of these stories

4.1. The woman that of being indebted and thrown of the house for not having how to pay, happened to earn 5000 dollars a week

Enriqueta, that's the woman's name. She did not work, she lived humbly with her husband and her two children, the husband worked in a warehouse and earned $ 450 a week, they managed to pass it by. Enriqueta attended to her children at home.

One bad day the husband was surprised by a fulminating heart attack that immediately ended his life. The owner of the warehouse where the man worked only helped with the expenses of the funeral and some dollars with what the family reached him for just over a month.

Two months later the woman was evicted for lack of payment and without even having anywhere to go was welcomed by a neighbor who clarified that he would help her only for a few days. The woman went out looking for work, found some cleanings that did not amount to $ 250 a week, but at least it was something.

One day one of her children brought her a piece of paper saying that at her school they would throw a goodbye party at the end of the year and that everyone should bring something to share. Enriqueta, who could not spend more than 15 dollars, prepared a sweet cake for her son to take, all those who tried the cake were delighted and that was how Enriqueta's story began.

To this day she has custom-made sweet cake every day to more than 50 stores in the city. Make each cake to split into 25 pieces to each business, for which they give you 20 dollars for each cake. He has employees who help him get the job done and his life changes completely.

4.2. Create your own marketing network

The marketing networks are a very lucrative business for its founders and the first people that give it exit from its founders, then they become a chain of people who consume products, they buy them to stay in a system that will do very rich to another.

Most of their products are supplements that almost nobody is interested in buying and with an assessed price, but they sell you a dream to stay in it and recommend to others who will contribute to generate millions of sales that will make a company richer every day.

However, if you create your own network with the products that are really consumed every day, everyone will be willing to buy, since its use is mandatory, at the same time that it helps them earn money to consume.

The products of daily consumption, food, cleaning, daily routine, coffee, tea, etc. They arrive at the distributor with a margin of 30% of profit for those who distribute it.

If you join a group of people who want to progress together with you and create a cooperative winery where they sell those products at the same market price, but only earning 10% for you and in another 20% from a network of affiliates and referrals between 10 % in a first level, 5% in a second level and 5% in a third level, you can be sure that in a short time the whole city will be buying in your warehouse.

While consumers buy the obligatory products at the same price of the whole market, earn money for talking about your business and refer others, all will have very good profits. Can you imagine that they can sell three million monthly with a 10% profit for you?

4.3. The teenager who unwittingly won a million dollars in a year selling postcards

What started as a game? A young girl took some posters of favorite characters from the internet to decorate her room, one day she was visited by a friend who was fascinated with the decoration, she asked her friend to take some out for her. The young woman who was not stupid immediately realized that it could be a business. He began to share his posters on social networks and ended up putting a store in the garage of his house to sell the posters, and then with the help of his mother they were placed in decoration stores and patented his business, after the first year they had sold 200 thousand posters at $ 5 each.

5. Exploit what you know

A woman tired of working in a nail center, one day decided to change her fatigue for intelligence. After arriving exhausted every day at home after long hours of work, he had a great idea.

She went out to investigate several beauty centers that did not have nail service, and she offered to do it, but not as an employee, if not taking the equipment, doing the work and paying a percentage of her earnings to the owner of the establishment.

He returned home and collected his savings that reached him to buy 6 computers. That same day, she posted a notice requesting employees with a high knowledge of nails, evaluated their candidates and chose the 6 best ones. He placed each one in a diferent establishment.

With the work of each, paid the owner of the establishment and the employee and had a good amount for her that multiplied 6 times were more than enough to cover their needs and keep investing, set as goal 100.

establishments, the year had already been achieved. Each employee of your business generates daily around 60 dollars net for her; if you notice 60x100 is 6000 dollars every day.

6. Offers a home service

We live in a time that what we most need is time. People do not like to make time anywhere, for example in the beauty salon.

Maria, thinking that very thing, without knowing anything about beauty, had the idea of creating little cards offering all the beauty services at home and took them to several places where women who have little time work. Banks, clinics, etc.

Hired beauty specialists who were unemployed and working for appointments, more than 50 clients a day request their service. Maria only pays a percentage of the work to the employee, does not consume electricity, does not pay for local service and also gives the option to her clients to sell the product lines.

As you can tell, it only needs a great idea, with what you know how to do or what you are willing to do and materialize your idea. Clean wealth is not magic, it is the result of good work and great effort.

Move away from you people who approach you to offer you riches that can only materialize in the imagination, there are many sellers of dreams that ultimately only enslave you for the dreams of others and yours will never be realized or need to be an old man waiting for that to happen. What is the use of wealth when you are 80?

7. The 3 unique tips for acquiring Wealth:

Producer's mentality

You must make great changes of thought to move from consumer to producer.

Some examples: consumers eat pizza, producers make pizza; consumers watch movies, producers make movies; consumers look for work, producers give work. And only the producers get rich.

If you study millionaires closely, you will see that most of them deliver a valuable service to millions of people. The question is what do you do every day to increase the value of your workday. If you make 10 sales calls per day, try to increase them. If you care for a child, try opening a daycare. And of course, not by working more cuts the quality of your services.

Just do millionaire activities

One of the things that kills a person's wealth faster is that it stays in a place of poverty. Many times, human beings place themselves in places filled with poor people.

Use your talents

We all have natural talents. Some people have a lot, while others stand out in one. No matter what your case may be, you must use what was given to you. The money is printed every day for you. Make sure you take what belongs to you.

Money is a tool that will allow you to dedicate yourself to what you like most. Stop "survive" and start to "live".

8. Create a product

The creation of a product and subsequent sale of it is another way to make money. One of the biggest mistakes that aspiring inventors make is not to evaluate the demand that may exist for their possible creation. Before developing the products you should talk to potential prospects to see the market up close.

Many aspire to become millionaires, but not all are prepared to devote the necessary energy and change their way of thinking to achieve their goal. In a world where being a millionaire is the new goal for the richest, becoming a millionaire is a real possibility and to achieve it you need good management, intelligent thinking and occasional calculated risks.

You will not become a millionaire sitting down and wishing that the money comes to your life or playing the lottery every week, nor will it happen if you only read about how to get it. Once you know which tools to use and which way of thinking to adopt, the rest of the real effort is to do something concrete to achieve that goal.

9. You must value your abilities

Billionaire Jack Ma, the founder of Alibaba, revealed that he even did poorly in a job interview of 25 candidates and only 1 rejection, but he always had the confidence to be the best.

Regardless of how others evaluate your abilities, you can become a millionaire as long as you do not join the complaints and finally stop complaining or easily take advantage of an opportunity.

10. Be tenacious.

To be successful you have to have the ability to get up after failing. You will find many failures in your way as you look for better ways to earn 1 million. It is not a matter of having the security of an average salary and your boss's orders every day.

To become a millionaire, you must be prepared to make decisions that will not always be successful, but if you do not take risks, you will not know their potential good results.

If you assume and put into practice the tips and intrusions presented here, you will be rich in no more than one year.

SUCCESS DEPENDS ON YOU, IF YOU PURSUE IT AND FIGHT TO HURT IT, YOU WILL HAVE IT IN YOUR HANDS..............................

www.ingramcontent.com/pod-product-compliance
Lightning Source LLC
Chambersburg PA
CBHW032311240526
45464CB00023BA/2990